Local Honey

ROBERT SAXTON was born in Nottingham in 1952 and now lives in north London, where he is the editorial director of an illustrated book publishing company. His first collection of poetry, *The Promise Clinic*, was published by Enitharmon Press in 1994; his second, *Manganese*, appeared from Carcanet Press/Oxford*Poets* in 2003. He is also represented in Faber's *Poetry Introduction 7* and the Carcanet/Oxford*Poets* anthology *Oxford Poets 2001*. In 2001 he won the Keats–Shelley Memorial Association's poetry prize for 'The Nightingale Broadcasts'. Robert Saxton's website may be visited at www.robertsaxton.co.uk.

T0154907

also by Robert Saxton from Carcanet Press / Oxford*Poets*

Manganese

ROBERT SAXTON

Local Honey

Oxford*Poets*

CARCANET

First published in Great Britain in 2007 by
Carcanet Press Limited
Alliance House
Cross Street
Manchester M2 7AQ

A CIP catalogue record for this book is available from the British Library
ISBN 978 1 903039 90 8

The publisher acknowledges financial assistance from Arts Council England

Typeset by XL Publishing Services, Tiverton
Printed and bound in England by SRP Ltd, Exeter

in memory of
Joyce Saxton (1920–2005)

Acknowledgements

Thanks are due to the editors of the following publications in which some of these poems first appeared:
Damn the Caesars, PN Review, Poetry London, Shearsman, Times Literary Supplement.

The last three lines of 'Half-lives' are borrowed, not quite verbatim, from Roger Scruton, *Modern Philosophy* (Sinclair-Stevenson, London 1994; Random House (Arrow), London 1997).

'Local Honey' and 'Tanging the Swarm' are indebted to Eva Crane, *The World History of Beekeeping and Honey Hunting* (Duckworth, London 1999).

The last three lines of 'The New Life' are the envoi of D.G. Rossetti's version of a sestina by Dante, collected with his translation of *La Vita Nuova* (*New York Review of Books*, New York 2002).

'The Quilting Bee' was awarded a commendation in the National Poetry Competition 2005.

'Earth Life' is indebted to Chayim Bloch, *Golem: Legends of the Ghetto of Prague*, 1919 (translated by Harry Schneiderman, Vienna 1925; facsimile edition Kessinger, Whitefish MT 1997).

The refrain of 'Double Trouble' was inspired by a Mose Allison blues, 'Days Like This' (on the album *The Word from Mose*, Atlantic 1964).

Contents

Moon Harvest

A Starfish on the Lawn

Half-lives

When mind and sky were twinned,
    everything fell into place:
shy edges, fear behind,
      this cave that feels like home,
the intuition of the face,
guessing what fingers trace
      of mind's neglected bloom.

Just so we trace our selves
    and fill a cave-wall diary
with the habits of wolves,
      tricked into heart's lair
for the evening bestiary,
tomorrow's archery,
      feathered like a prayer.

Bright words come next, like blades,
    which flash from sleep to sleep,
slice twilight into shades.
      With mouths we understand,
roaming the tall and deep,
those wolves that look like sheep,
      that whale confused with land.

Some animals we've caught
    and bred to bark at flies.
Meanwhile a strange, bad thought
      troubles us, our every wrong
seen through a dog's eyes,
sharp, creaturely surmise,
      witness with future tongue.

Long arrows that we loose
    like selfish prayers fall short.
Our best words reproduce,
        angels in flying school.
To say what makes one thought
true is to express a thought –
      the *same* thought, as a rule.

Black Holes

No hot coals
    in twilit golf
will help players tee
    on sight
any of their lost balls,
    dark trysts
being scarcely right
    for serious play.

Three bright moles
    fox a wolf
above, safe in a tree
    where its tight
cage of roots convulses
    in twists
of midnight,
    and blind as clay.

The black holes
    of the self
where we'll never see
    the light
are to everyone else
    the fists
they have to fight,
    and clear as day.

Bishop's Rock

Britain's westernmost lighthouse, Isles of Scilly; automated 1991

Lighthouses remember
    themselves manned,
obviously. This one's
    a lonely blind
colossus with the leaky roof
    of the mind
on its shoulders, still heroic,
    hardly bland,

and still, I'm sure,
    believing shipwreck
averted, a vessel
    wished back to its dock
by a mind going mad
    on Bishop's Rock,
a rabid sailor
    drowning on the deck.

Paradise Lost

'The little dogs and all, Tray, Blanch, and Sweetheart, see, they bark at me.'
King Lear, III.vi

The Devil rides out
    to the flooded hive.

'Man and his dog,
    in The Alcazar.'

Just one last wish:
    a dream, a star.

Scooterman say,
    You drink, I drive.

      ***

'You're jesting, sir?
    Its name is Tray?

Dog people know
    you call a pup

by a name no dog
    could muddle up

with a key command,
    like Sit or Stay.'

      ***

To wish the wish
    the Devil's guessed

is pure abasement,
    drink your fill,

your karmic rating
less than nil.

Scooterman know
that he know best.

Voyaging

Seas are where you recognise
the pirates, or the flock or school
whose harsh yet neighbourly cries
lash a comfortable ridicule,

fins ploughing clay, turning the worm,
gulls nimble as English men-o'-war,
a buoy bolt-upright in the storm,
which then turns out to be more

like a weathercock, then indeed
a weathercock, on a drowned spire
undaunted by a white horse stampede,
or loss of the uplifting choir

damned by raiding pagan gospels.
Only oceans have cathedrals.

***

Woods are what vandals left behind
when carrying off the history prize.
They float like pondweed on the mind.
Their leaves are the republic's lies,

and grandma's hairnet, smiling gold,
all weathers' topsail, crow's-nest of straw.
She keeps the girls from growing old,
which keeps the boys from wanting more.

Virtue is cheeky, villainy po-faced,
luxury a mask, poverty a root.
This dry log's lettering in a rustic taste
charts sea-lanes blossoming with loot.

Forests are the limbo of the hatless drowned,
failed baptism, the stonefish wound.

The Fair Maid of Kent

I discovered one incredible year –
    the year of my transformation –
    that every half-way decent thought
    I'd had, and buffed up as my own,
    and scribbled into my private notebook,
    someone had had and honed and told the world before:
Rabindranath Tagore.

When after six months of servitude
    I shrugged off the albatross
    of a possessive fiancée and set sail
    for a new life in the Antipodes,
    hearing those timbers creak I didn't care
    that I was sea-sick, alone and far from shore:
I'd tasted fresh air and wanted more.

'The soil in return for her service
    keeps the tree tied to her, while the sky,
    asking nothing, allows it to be free.'
    The captain, seeing that the passage he'd marked
    in his book of meditations had thrown me
    into a reverie, banged his cane on the cabin floor.
'Rabindranath Tagore,'

he said, then smiled. And the ship, in which that tree
    seemed crucified for all our freedom's
    sake, was gaoler and prisoner of the wind,
    and puking over its side I saw
    upside-down its name, *The Fair Maid of Kent,*
    in gold script on the bow,
which made me feel more myself somehow.

Why I Never Write on My Hand

I can't write in the books I read,
annotating like some needy autodidact.
       I just can't.
Nor can I write on my hand –
a phone number, a recipe, a bon mot.
Better to take in information thoroughly,
       deep inside oneself,
instead of leaving it floating on the surface
       like quayside litter.

You've made a cabinet of your head.
You won't quench your thirst because your cup's cracked.
       You're a saint
in your own suburb of sand.
Why shut yourself away from the flow
of the mind's making? – it's always messy
       at the edge of the self.
There's beauty, sometimes, in an ailing trace.
       Catch it, make it better.

Then let common sense be the cure.
We share a book with its conjuring mind,
       the magus on stage
whose absorption warrants our silence.
Not so different is a stranger's right
not to have to wonder about
       hieroglyphics,
a public skin with a private blemish,
       a thought where a thought shouldn't be.

You've swallowed the dazzling lure
and the barbed hook behind.
       Keeping the page
as it came off the press is a violence
against nature, a fist held tight
around its dust, without

the endearing fix,
nor any mark of age, memory or wish –
a lie in its purity.

Manners is no lie – wild ink impedes
the quiet consensual flow.

My number's in the book nobody reads.
Write yours, if you will, below:

Groundhuggers

Singed hair grows proudest in the underclass.
A step's advantage makes each nuance gross.
I'm looking low, intention rum, eyes close.

Rough rebel courtiers grace the rabbit king.
One lives, but only just, and mourns his tongue.
Nine thrive, in warrens, like the Viet Cong.

We veterans mint the medal in the scar,
scratch beer from sand, loathe passers-by,
piss from the terrace with its false view of sky

where gormless gorgons calcify the dawn,
numbing the sprightliest verb to starchiest noun,
the shooting party clueless on the down.

The Song of Situations

Mind's a river, never empty,
tree forgets while axe remembers,
skies make far from easy walking,
friends flow on when sorrows whisper,

tree forgets while axe remembers,
even tigers have their off-days,
friends flow on when sorrows whisper,
like the rainbow no one noticed,

even tigers have their off-days,
on the delta's lazy steamboat,
like the rainbow no one noticed,
gambling, loving, cheating, losing,

on the delta's lazy steamboat,
strangers annotate their purpose,
gambling, loving, cheating, losing,
one may one day be your saviour,

strangers annotate their purpose,
parrots parody the moment,
one may one day be your saviour,
champion of the clouds' regatta,

parrots parody the moment,
skies make far from easy walking,
champion of the clouds' regatta,
mind's a river, never empty.

The Flute Player

after Rumi

The flute
dismays
three birds

all sad
to hear
such cries

for its
dear nest
so far

away,
its bed
of reeds,

since they
had hoped
to hear

instead
how breath
can make

you see
a man
whose heart

throbs like
a bird,
showing

such skill
breath hops
with joy,

song-flight
of all
he loves

and not
nine holes
of pain,

deep wish
to fly
back home,

though both
clipped wings
and all

free breath
just tell
you this:

he's lost,
hollow,
empty,

farther
from the
source than

ever –
whence all
music.

Tanging the Swarm

Some of us do acrobatics
   in the bone's arena,
some are gaolers of the landscape's
   prison, like a rheumatic's
grumbling subpoena,
   others are shadowy shapes
like ghosts in fake photos
   of the late honey flows.

Medium-weight colonies
   hereabouts are over–
wintered, while the rest
   are killed like flies,
but with more palaver,
   in an Oktoberfest
of toxic puffball smoke
   wafted by the keeper's cloak.

The heaviest yield ecstasy,
   the lightest would never
have survived anyway.
   A summer of celibacy
ripens love's fever,
   deciduous foreplay,
merry-go-round of weasels
   where the honey drizzles.

***

'Bees delight,' said Plato,
   'in the clash and clang of bronze' –
though lacking any organ like the ear.
   Tanging is a loud farrago,
a beating of sticks on pans
   that somehow keeps bees near,
settling as a sticky swarm
   far from the trumped-up storm –

near home, in fact, though
     sometimes the trick will fail
and the swarm give you chase
     over hill and hollow
like a fox looping its trail
     to throw you off its case,
evacuating boundaries,
     inkjet of legal quandaries,

buzzing over rivers
     without regard to fords
and into a majestic park
     of lawns and cedars
and ornamental herds
     of goats, then, behind a dark
hedge, pink roses
     where a coy dryad poses.

***

Some of us are chemical
     in the bone's alembic
or the fleas of the alchemist
     dark and hunched, all
of us riding the thick
     vapours where they twist
to the shape of your desire,
     honey from the secret shire.

Since a swarm is deemed a chattel
     of the owner of the hive,
tanging serves a brave purpose,
     like a drum in a battle,
announcing, *J'arrive!*,
     the beekeeper breathless,
trespassing but sorry
     in pursuit of his quarry.

Some throwback of the night
    has tried to expand
this notion to aver
    that tanging secures the right
to roam anyone's land
    where your swarm's astir.
Thus the rationalist schemes.
    In your dreams, in your dreams!

Local Honey

On Lüneberg Heath

To be a bee churl with no money,
 only taxable bees,
 isn't the worst fate
 imaginable
 on Lüneberg Heath.
You could pay the tax with honey,

take the bees to the heather,
 milk the late honey flows,
 set the skeps on straw
 and push straw gently
 up against the combs
with the onset of colder weather.

Calluna, Calluna

The summers are silent and the winters long.
 It takes a lifetime wishing on the wing
  to separate the heather from the ling.

Only a native in a native song
 can separate the heather from the ling –
  so let's unpack our saddlebags and sing,

jostle fresh air in a languid lung,
 let a few late stray bees accompany our song,
  and separate the heather from the ling.

The Impossible Goodbye

Alone with Angie's Macaw

Feeding willow branches from the landing
    through the open door into the spare room,
like pushing brushwood into a furnace,
    in a biker's helmet with fiery dragon-scales

swept back from both sides of the visor,
    flame-like, Valkyrie-like,
I'm hating it, and almost hating her –
    and all for those ribbons of loose talk,

mad squawks her pet-names might be rescued
    from and brandished to disarm,
or some dark secret stolen from its blackmailer,
    or even the most romantic phrase

she ever heard, sicked up repeatedly –
    imagine how her ice-fastness might fall
on hearing this spoken low, and serious,
    and once, by such a focused friend as me.

Vertigo

Illiteracy can't quench a *real* star.
    Paparazzi blaze the bush but not the root.
You know exactly where your exes are –
    or where the footprint lurks, if not the foot.
Like a freed slave who one day wakes up singing
you shower in ass's milk, eyes stinging,
                and find
                each wind
convenient for dress and hair, body and mind.

Anyone with eternity in their sights
    will know the more you read the less you'll see.
Reserve your friendships for the darkest nights.
    Dismiss the Southern Belle (she tolls for thee) –
that snake-oil doc who diagnosed ME.
No decent stud donates his sperm for free.
                You'd swear,
                nowhere
in the world but in your bed is poker fair.

An ungiftwrapped word you're pleased to know,
    rolled around your mouth like a sweet,
melts me – honestly. It's vertigo.
    Some lookalike you wanted me to meet,
blonde body-double dizzier when I met her,
invisible ink beside your loveless letter,
                star she
                won't be.
For your one letter now I've written three.

When I come close,
    you blur –
which means
    I'll never see you

close enough
    to carry back
from where we go
    to where we always

should have stayed
    the thing
we wish for,

    fine and clear –
only, vaguely,
    the thing we fear.

Cloud Nine

In a folly too close to the house,
   a walkover like a turf maze
unlikely to be lost in haze,
   I hang around the Grecian frieze
balloon garlands antique air sways,
   trembling like an antique phrase.

This evening, my pipistrelle,
   the Tempietto on the grassy knoll,
secret objective of your stroll,
   flourishes a proud singleton,
its finial, a Grecian urn,
   to mark the point of no return.

Balloon bouquets in sanctum's heat,
   each with acanthus counterpart,
welcome of my expectant heart,
   release the ruby from its ore,
decking a party in its lair
   with double balls and sheaths of air.

'A motto ennobles the resolute.'
   Liking my destiny ornate,
I'll carve a volute if she's late,
   let others mop or map their stains,
inflate their fears, lullaby bones,
   weigh bubbles on a scale of stones.

I'll carve a volute if she's late,
   bent like some patient anchorite
whose eyebrows knit by candlelight,
   a white slave in a tyrant's mine
conjuring from the coal, at noon,
   trusting, our glint of honeymoon.

Sixty balloons hold their surprise
    like breath I'm saving to propose,
a poem that endstops miles of prose,
    an antic wood, acanthus-leaved,
the folly not too far removed
    from the ballroom where she was loved.

November Wedding

Confetti, we presume, is banned:
      there's no space for a brush
between the rows of grand
      tombs in their commuters' crush,
and a garden vac might swallow
      up a ghost, or its hellish din
evict one from its sleepy hollow,
      torn from more soundly sleeping kin –

or has the mischief in each guest
      been exorcised by the snow shower
with which the heavens have blessed
      your bride in her most public hour,
muting first with lacy drapes
      the colours of things the snow falls on
but leaves as shapes,
      for softening later, guests all gone?

Spring Motor Tour

In the handbook there was no reference
        to the correct pressures for the tyres,
so judging the matter by eye I pumped them
        just hard enough not to bulge
any more, then off we flew, motoring
        through the blossom-heavy shires,
prising apart every shady secret
        our *Shell Guide* was proud to divulge –

an underground ballroom, an ex-Crusader's
        folly with a fake minaret
where three Catholic children for two years
        found sanctuary from the violence
of the age. By the time our breakfast toast arrived,
        we'd almost agreed to forget
our night of trials and talks, each of us cradling
        with helpless arms the other's inexperience.

With its half-scripted adventures a new day
        stretched before us, breezy and wholesome.
We motored through beguiling woods,
        on the lookout for the telltale signs
our guidebook promised – tacitly accepting
        that any serious effort to explore

what might become of our marriage was better made within
        a framework of routine. Only after getting back home
and thoroughly washing the car did I finally come across
        the tyre pressure guidelines
on a printed metal platelet riveted to the outer edge
        of the driver's door.

Bialowieza Honeymoon

Five woodpeckers – middle spotted, black,
   white-backed, grey-headed, three-toed – flit
among the wildwood, soft as rain.
   Their tomtoms dope our native wit,
leaving us speechless, miles off-track.
   A twig lets off a deafening crack.
      Spell broken, who'll re-weave it?

The wolf-cubs weeping in the cull,
   the milkmaid flouncing, proud to quit.
Our afternoon's a pile of coins
   like last year's leaves – the blackbird's writ.
At least with you life's never dull,
   or won't be, with your milking stool.
      What? Left it behind? Retrieve it!

More beetroot soup, with cubes of toast.
   Only one lamp in three is lit.
The airship drops its dump of mail.
   The cuckoo chick, giant counterfeit,
brainwashes its warbler host,
   the banquet's meek exhausted ghost
      whose wiring cries, Believe it!

Black sausage, pea-green casserole,
   salad of dock, with cuckoo-spit,
for afters just a heap of nuts.
   A serious citrus deficit.
Well-fed, the pygmy owl patrol
   checks the cassette player, psychs its goal –
      one night they might achieve it.

The wryneck in the Palace Park,
   the bear-queen sulking in her pit.
Our honeymoon's a crock of gold,
   a file that makes the pieces fit.
My Mockney winking in the dark
   tickles your fancy, flints a spark.
      Well, would you Adam 'n' Eve it?

Strangers on a Train

The wilderness seeds itself everywhere,
the incoming tide, breathed out again
in the dreams we make almost true.
Give up a living moment you can spare,
perhaps to a child you've just met on a train
who needs it least and loves it less than you.

Often, at least, I did my best to share,
claim half the seeds and think of these as main,
yet fling both lots like this child at a zoo,
mixing together on a falling tide of air.
It was a good living, just waiting for rain.
Only in dreams did just my own crop push through.

In other dreams my weather swung from fair
to full, the least breeze adding to the trees' pain
and dressing with living clouds the mortal blue.
I woke to all the seeds left in my care,
impatient like time and tide, whose vast plain
sail thrills a child as much as any storm's brew.

Each conquest was an unborn child's flare
launched from its cell of dreams, nature's campaign
to topple the future's tide in a bloodless coup.
The least loved found my shade, the most my glare.
In every loss I saw the seeds of gain,
a million living feet for every shoe.

No living room's too small for that one square
meal no child of mine would dare disdain,
a snack of seeds, an elastic curfew,
breakfast of wholesome dreams we might compare,
then flush away least harmful to the drain
and, later, to the tide's sincere adieux.

The retreating tide of every failed affair
left living debris, a beautiful stain
that mapped, sketchily at least, my due,
where the child who chose to be my heir
rode down the delta of dreams, the soft refrain
of seeds, making the tunnel safe, for all I knew.

My seeds, in dreams at least, fly with your grain.
A child will box the tide, smash earth's taboo.
You love the living dark, and the dark loves you.

Clementine

Sands of the desert crowned you,
   slaking their thirst in your own way,
      drifting to beauty's laws.

In an orange-grove I found you,
   lantern of shortening day,
      calling through palace doors,

ajar, my love wrapped around you,
   so easily pulled away,
      like a dress, but always yours.

Bird Song

The goldcrest flock,
    the mistle thrush.

The routine of increase,
    the storm warning.

A campfire
    in a nest of sorrow.
Wise I'd be
    to start to grieve,
if not today
    perhaps tomorrow –

even while
    my bridges burn.

I speak the language
    of the beech woods.

My every wish
    is already a regret.

You speak the language
    of the pine woods.

Your word for 'still'
    is the same

as your word for 'yet'.

Your love for me
    is a poor sparrow,
in the bedroom
    of your sleeve.
It's with a word
    as with an arrow:

once let loose
    it won't return.

Magpie Minstrel Valentine

I stole the magpie's ring one day,
    I'd planned this raid for ages,
and somehow came to have my way
    by weathering her rages.

The robin hopped around my spade
    and warned me of disaster.
I blushed deep red, the robin's shade,
    and started digging faster.

Things make no sense in black and white,
    I've only time for rainbows.
Her ring sits on my finger tight
    and through its hoop my pain flows

till black is white and white is crap
    and rainbow's lost its reason.
The mice are nibbling round the trap
    whose spike still has its cheese on.

Things make no sense in black and white,
    at dominoes I'm useless.
Her ring sits on my finger tight,
    my circulation's juiceless.

The magpie hunts in Tudor Close
    while I hunt in The Birches.
Just down one small addictive dose
    and love will gain its purchase.

The magpie steals from Tudor Way
    while I steal from The Beeches.
Minstrel, you take my breath away
    and drain my blood with leeches.

Your song's a stack of broken light,
    a vandalised piano,
the zebra–fish my anthracite,
    its flame my golden minnow.

The magpie roosts in Tudor Drive
    while I roost in The Cedars.
The heart that's keeping us alive
    's the hand that fails to feed us.

The magpie's drawn to all that shines
    and drops it in her bling sack.
She doesn't care for Valentines
    and doesn't want her ring back.

The New Life

*To the Lady Pietra degli Scrovigni –
from a Florentine in exile*

I stepped out of my hut into your shade
like a shy ragtag shepherd of the hills.
My days being invisible, blended with grass,
unmerry-go-round of work against the green,
a rosary of servitude for a soul of stone,
I'd dreamed of sheep, never of any lady.

Then a lad in the village spied a lady
one day, while conkering in a chestnut's shade.
Spilling his tale, he swore it on a stone,
so by nightfall all the people of the hills
knew that a lady on the village green
had woven for herself a coronet of grass,

and seeming not to care about the grass
stains on her dress this fine and feisty lady
sat for an hour, softly singing 'Green-
sleeves'. Then, rising, like a blissful shade
of paradise she floated towards the hills,
miraculously hovering right over the stone

circle of Fiesole whose every stone
announces to us that our lives are grass.
This brought to me new purpose in the hills.
Every sheep bleated that I'd never find my lady,
but years of searching every patch of shade
and sun in camouflage of dark and pale green

have proved them wrong: where sheep see only green,
I see that I've just missed you. Sure as stone,
the whisper of your passage, like shade
chasing its cloud across the rippling grass,
is a message dropped to me from my lady –
the scent and warmth and light of Tuscan hills.

In middle age I'm happy in these hills.
I have your company, and though I'm not green
enough to think I'll ever know my lady –
I'm just a shepherd after all, and a stone'
s throw's closer than shepherds get to heaven's grass –
from paradise I summon Dante's shade:

'However dark the hills throw out their shade,
under her summer's green the beautiful lady
covers it, like a stone covered in grass.'

Jason and the Argonauts

A kind of gypsy band
    in southwest Morocco,
refugees from Samarkand
    with fractious goats in tow,
despising the life of ease
    in cushioned kasbahs,
sleep among argan trees
    beneath the wandering stars.

Skinny, shaggy and spry,
    these goats love nothing more
than to clamber up high
    into the treetop store
of an argan tree, to graze
    on the olive-like flesh
of its fruits, which folk praise
    from Fez to Marrakech.

Each fruit conceals a prize –
    for *people*, that is: three
kernels, whose shell defies
    the goats' gastrology.
Spiralling, outward-bound,
    unsheathed it drops,
cryptic, wrinkled and round,
    in the shade of an argan copse.

And this is where the women come
    harvesting, from dark bazaars,
as if to compute the sum
    of all their luckless stars
on the abacus of nuts
    vouchsafed from humble heights,
pearls from goats' guts,
    like tiny meteorites.

Later they break the shells
    open with a stone tool
to liberate the kernels,
    which they roast, then, when cool,
rotate by camel power
    in a quern, grindingly slow,
till ground as fine as flour,
    then mix with water to a dough.

Then in an argan-wood press
    shined by fingers they toil
with strength, and gentleness,
    to extract the argan oil,
loved for its dark, nutty taste,
    olfactory flowers,
the slightest love-lines traced
    in a poet's loneliest hours.

Accept, now, this caprice
    from a gypsy of the heart,
a goat shorn of its fleece,
    toiling, hopeful, apart
in the desert of a book
    whose evening sweats a smile,
a drop of argan oil. Look.
    Please find attached, this phial.

Worpington Hall

Two Spells

Breakfast Spell

Wishes with addresses,
    dieting to be posted,
sober vagrant guesses
    in the gutter, wasted,

some signed up to cruises
    only snobs resisted,
winners backing losers,
    nuisances accosted,

steaming open letters
    archivists have listed,
creditors' and debtors',
    copperplate, ham-fisted,

others snorting roses
    equerries have tested,
rhetoric of noses
    while their summer lasted –

wishes with addresses
    fading as they fasted,
kept alive by stresses,
    every morning, toasted.

Supper Spell

Aggravated losses,
    all the traps you trusted,
slap-downs from your bosses,
    torched and served with mustard,

ever finer messes
    brightest boots resisted,
hasty, blushing yesses
    senior vision misted,

non-prescription glasses –
    pudding, vodka, custard –
worth a million masses,
    spies who loved you lusted,

backstage wet with kisses,
    virgin soap queen boasted,
circle loud with hisses,
    time a star was rested,

freeze the moment's juices,
    next day's talents ghosted,
activate your mooses,
    in the oven, roasted.

The Goatherd

The Liffey rang last orders in the night.
Across the Halfpenny Bridge he piped his goat.
Pub crawlers noted nothing of any note.

The gypsy princess on her barge of state
was fishing with a safety-pin for trout,
her bait a maggot liquoriced in stout.

Across the Halfpenny Bridge he piped his goat.
The gypsy princess on her barge of state,
where Egypt's wobbliest sailors navigate

the wildest waves, noted nothing of any note –
only the drunken reel of a flashlight
high above her prospecting the velvet night

for jewels, the trade winds swollen with stout,
and cross-currents of educated debate
in honour of dark Cleopatra lying in state

below the Halfpenny Bridge, so late.

Well shy of the crowd,
set on a hard hat,
pink with a lime-green peak,
two full horns of ale
drain in through a pair of tubes
with a join at the mouth.

Hey, this beer's not right –
too thin, flat and warm!
But the race can't start
till the whole lot's drunk
so a proud thirst grins,
then it's down in one.

Then a gun goes bang
and a horse drops dead –
no, that's just a joke.
Then a gun goes bang
and the whole field's off
while your nerves pump hard.

And half this lot's sick
as they lose their shirt –
the half full of hate
when the horns get filled
up with two more pints
by a toff in a bib

when a dud romps home.

Scouting for Lovers

At night in woods where lovers are thought to be present,
    bear in mind the constellations will be partially obscured
    by branches in winter, by the leaf canopy in summer,
    and you cannot be certain you will not lose your way.

When striving to acquaint yourself with constellation fragments,
    practise by placing intricate cardboard cutouts of trees
    over your star map – you will soon learn to recognise
    Orion without his belt, Andromeda without her girdle.

At night in woods where lovers may be on the move,
    remember that no twig snaps without good reason;
    also, that a couple is likely to maintain communication
    by occasionally giving the call of their patrol animal.

Study hedgehogs, badgers, foxes and the like,
    their cries, purrs and gasps, their odd little clicks –
    without such knowledge scoutcraft is incomplete.
    Equally, learn their habits – hedgehog, inventor of fire,

of the prickly flush on a lover's throat, rolling among fruits,
    returning with apples to its young in a hollow tree,
    badger drumming on its stomach at full moon,
    or disguised as a monk to promote its insatiable appetites,

fox changing into a young man to entice a woman,
    or a woman to entice a young man, or greeting the sunrise
    by kneeling on its hindlegs and stretching its forelegs
    on the ground – easily mistaken for your scoutmaster.

The Passion

An appreciation society

The emu's the Mazda of meat, olé,
and the lion's the chicken of choice.
      But good butchers agree,
      and they'll tell you for free,
that the ortolan bird's the Rolls Royce.

(Or just *ortolan*, I more strictly should say –
to be picky, the 'bird' here's redundant.)
      So we're setting the traps,
      and great minds need no maps,
for the ortolan's truly abundant –

though we're making it rarer, and upping the odds,
and the point's the most marvellous hunting.
      (By the way, I might add,
      it'll make your heart glad,
that the ortolan's my favourite bunting.)

Yes, we're making it rarer, the food of the gods,
while enjoying the most glorious hunting.
      And it's more than a fad –
      it's a passion, a jihad,
on behalf of the ortolan bunting.

The Quilting Bee

WELL DRESSERS can be surprisingly cynical,
      jeering at any elations that make the gloom rise.
Look for:
      pickpocketing, glove snipping, button theft,
      hat spoiling, fragrant evasion of bosom tax.

WILL WITNESSES will occasionally bring back
      a few viviparous jokes from the intestate beyond.
Look for:
      rare mischief lights in the eyes,
      quadruple handshakes, crypto-Calvinist soliloquies.

JOY RIDERS peddle a popular Algerian adrenaline therapy
      based on asymmetric speed breathing.
Look for:
      second-hand airbags, unidentifiable rattles,
      foxing in the margins of service records.

JAY WALKERS are seldom insouciant, many having actuarial
      degrees and student endowment loans with mutual widows.
Look for:
      whistling of yesterday's jingles, titanium jaw work,
      peripheral fringing of self-awareness.

CHUTE PACKERS are unregulated but conscientious,
      mindful of hogging searchlights by proxy.
Look for:
      unassertive handkerchief origami,
      scorch offences, piracy over the high seas.

SHEET METALWORKERS enjoy wish-fulfilment,
      the wrap-around merchandising of cartoon characters.
Look for:
      lightning, time warps, contraband biscuits,
      outbreaks of Malaysian shadow puppetry.

The Queen's Reader

The Queen can no more read
    all the books
she receives as gifts
    than she can pause mid-hunt
to count the rebel rooks
    plotting in their windy lofts –

so a Reader offers
    from his dungeon of light
a stirrup for the royal brain,
    for sovereignty's sake,
a better-favoured height,
    enlarging its terrain

though not its power –
    which makes his head
a little like the fox
    within the breath of the pack,
being too well-read,
    or else, near traps, the rooks.

Fireman's Lift

The Thames is on fire – that is to say, timber,
    sails, rigging, jute, a ton of fresh gazettes,
and the occasional fireman's beard,
    like a burning bush among the firemen
brawling over every square yard of wharf,
    in rival teams competing for the fire,
or fighting off the Admiralty press-gang
    attracted by any such commotion; or

scarcely a London mile away, look! –
    the agony of the Opera House ablaze
in its Twilight of the Gods, and plain as Punch
    the firemen bribed to aim their hoses wide,
or even to take a wrong turn off Fleet Street,
    as if this fiery beacon weren't so obvious,
by a jealous diva, would-be or arrived, or a craven
    manager flushing his phantom out –

so that any hopeful soul shown around heaven
    by one of the old hands entrusted
with this duty (Nelson, say, or Dante),
    looking down, might learn that this is
just the kind of mess that press-gangs ghosts,
    men who die unshriven in naval battles,
or in the siege of a dressing room, or women
    embracing limelight, top notes and flames

in their *Liebestod*, and firemen, of course,
    a few rotten apples, including that lazy one
in the brothel, asleep in his rum-soaked shirt,
    who should be striding through the fire
with the harbourmaster's daughter in his arms,
    or leading her down a blazing staircase
out of the inferno, her nightdress billowing back
    in the updraught, unscathed like an angel's wings.

His Piano the Sea

Let this old lag audition your mulch –
he's an admiral, on leave, at home,
seasoned in the ebb and salt of years.
Where beechmast drifts like a cabinboy's
lies, hawfinches tack their livelihood.
Widows are careless with their wills,
children convinced his beard conceals gills.
The needle swings to rising damp,
scree rattles down the chimney, fast.

He chases the verdigris off protocol,
touching meat before money, wood before
wet. He has ten daughters, whom he charms
from every port, like a whispered salute
to the fishing fleet, 'God preserve you.'
He trusts the serious language of flags,
dresses freed slaves in old admiralty rags.
Each slap that perks and dies on the bow
confers merit. He knows the Windwards'

and Leewards' riptides, which badgers make
the finest sporrans, and how off Celtic
shores the seventh wave comes like a king
out of the cold, grey wastes, and hacks
at faith. The one bad apple's where grief starts –
the burning jetty, the perished cork,
the crabs, the plank, the widow's walk,
the oak-gall in the Book of Kells,
perils that anchor prayers to mud –

and yet for him the worst impediment's
only the wrong light in the cabin when
the sails are set, sick angels sweat in bed,
the staves are flatlining across their brains
and silence is a comma and sigh of hell
coiled in the ear of a nautilus shell,
bas clef, eyes lowered, on night's black loam,
those pale brown leaves like tiny hands.

Toy Story

If ever a soft toy's eyes were to come loose,
our governess would sew them tight again.
Her job's to rescue Punch from Judy's noose,

sort the clothespegs into men and women
singing, *Mares eat oats and does eat oats ...*
and later grace the grace with a soft amen.

She picks the naughtiest nits from velvet coats.
Gamely she jollies up our lady: 'Mink,
ermine, who needs 'em? Only minks and stoats.'

Then on her hobbyhorse in hunting pink
she's hunting down the fox who stole her pearls.
Flooded, the ballroom's a tip-top skating rink.

On skates, a lynx among delinquent girls,
Jill Frost between the lichened mirrors twirls.

Devil's Judge and Jury

Any judge who can steal the teeth from a kiss,
     the tithe of allpence-ha'penny from a purse
and the fierce red truth of love from a curse

qualifies, amply – welcome to this notorious case.
     Here's the file of all the jury's gutless pleas.
Here's the cell where they sleep and here's the keys.

Their first gambit is to demonstrate just cause.
     Count their days as weeks, their weeks as days.
Submit their limpness to the gorgon's gaze.

Tall dolls are the leverage you have on short guys
     who run the numbers for the lilywhite police.
Standards, loyalties, trust migrate like geese.

All Strasbourg now requires is an educated guess –
     far more humane than people's hit or miss.
But watch your mouth, your gold – gold digger's kiss.

The Travelling Naturalist

Xanadu

'In Xanadu the traffic lights are advisory,
window cleaners and chimney sweeps are redundant
and language is no longer the fuel of thought.'

In the long pause before the comedian's next observation
the audience's nervous fidgets could be heard distinctly.
A small cloud crossed the sun, briefly dimming the hall.

'A few brave souls have questioned whether
the restoration of the three surviving ruined academies
is the best possible use of available funds.'

At this point a veterinary student ran from her seat
and broke out noisily through the rear emergency exit
into a dark, insalubrious alleyway, exhausted and tearful.

'On arrival,' he continued after a coughing bout had subsided,
'you are given a *carnet*, a sheet sleeping bag and a timetable
of tides – which is also, of course, a lunar almanac.'

When a tweedy farmer guffawed in disbelief,
two seed suppliers in the row in front turned round to show him
such angry stares as might have sabotaged the Second Coming.

'Although yesterday's follies are tomorrow's grand houses,
the parvenu shows no impatience. All exercise is aerobic,
even bending down to free the slug from its beer-trap.'

Middle Earth

'A lady barrister fell in love with a man who had no jaw.
A replacement was grown on his shoulder-blade in a cage
of titanium mesh. A year later he could masticate again.'

The comedian stopped to pour himself some water –
the jug and glass were on a low table beside the lectern.
He took three slow sips, savouring them like wine.

'It was difficult, because for years he had nursed a passion –
unreturned – for a race-track designer, a millionairess. Perhaps
now was the time to start living at the business-end of devotion?'

Five latecomers, some of them with dried splashes of mud
on their clothing, slipped into an empty row near the back.
The whispered phrase, '…our Landrover…', explained everything.

'But let's get this into perspective. Hundreds of people are dying
daily here. To qualify as a doctor you have to study for
five, six, seven, eight years – even more to become a specialist.'

A few people were taking notes. Some – presumably
with permission – appeared to be recording the proceedings.
Two or three watch- or clock-watchers were tut-tutting a little.

'Yesterday's hardy sailors are tomorrow's lost souls,
their resilience pawned to pay for their care, their diaries
sub judice. Well-wishers lovingly log their voyages.'

Laputa

'This is the birth-shelf of hundreds of hitchhiker
origin myths. Fluffy turtles of the waterfront find landfall
as far away as Runcorn. An hour of booze has a fixed price.

'Here's a dentist's chair that sharpens the enjoyment
of a litre of cocktail. This is a volunteer patrolman coaxing
a lovemaking couple expertly away from turtles' eggs.'

Engrossed in the slide-show, they retreated into Adam's cave.
Beyond, on floods of light and silence, floated all imaginable fears.
An electric whirr kept language safe in its drainage channels.

'Seeking pleasure so urgently in the wrong places
causes serious collateral damage. Moon-starved hatchlings
row towards spectacular bar lights and drown in the sand.'

The comedian was distracted for a second or two –
there was dust in his water, backlit by the projector beam.
He smiled at his sister, exquisitely hatted in the side seats.

'The problem might call for drastic solutions, an aquarium,
or even a zoo – an ark with cabins for all of our hopes,
a dovecote aft, awaiting the return of compassion.

'But what of naturists who can't keep their binoculars steady?
The lover answers first because his blood's already moving:
"Clamp both hands around the peak of your baseball cap."'

The Ox Truck Prospectus

The one-step programme: remember, if someone
collapses you might have miles to drive.

We have not yet learned to speak from inside our
symptoms. You will be wise not to let the
vagueness of dreams fool you into mourning
them less as their smithereens settle and drift.
Join the club, the curve, the raffle and the
wound. Everyone we meet fields a different
adventure far beyond the crossroads of
our handshake.

Sticky the bee that drowns in mead, restless the new
century, gobbling history.

A faun has no business in a jam session: it's the
wrong kind of mischief. The Dorian mode is
scarcely for now – being mad, and made of
mud and *merde*. If your importance owes so
much to Viagra, it's a fine double bluff to
admit this to the princess. All decent ropes
have a brand, but the secret of social climbing
is
to celebrate false summits.

A bull in a field with a handkerchief on its horn. Trust and
silence go together like mistrust and silence.

Nothing but blue skies. Should we leave the little
cloud alone or call it Johnson? Within this
cocoon of noise there's a pregnant pause like a
silkworm inside the wardrobe of its palace,
uncertain whether to munch or spin, and so
doing neither. You are hiding here, with your
secret credentials, while your pipa player stalks
the dragon.

Why do lions' heads vomit water? They know you're
watching and they want to look busy.

In moss gardens tragedies compete with comedies.
    Swallowing designs on your daughter, showing
    off their veniality till it makes you dizzy and you
    look away, lions growl, which you take for
    the gurgling water. There's panic in the eyes of
    the owl, which also, and so wisely, loves your
    daughter – and you, for the hour's reprieve you've
    bought her.

Pedestrians on their own long leashes set coordinates
precisely, a minute ahead of the bra-hou-hou.

The east wind whips up leaves in your face and many
    who walk this way are scarred with cuts and
    careless of others' troubles. There was a little
    girl, moppeting from the purgatory of every
    thorn bush. Where Abstraction Street meets
    Attention Street I found evidence of errors
    aplenty but will cite only one: the skeleton of
    the strongman's greyhound.

Walking in your own footsteps requires extra food beyond
the competence of pilgrimage.

The first rough rub is the welcome starting to wear.
    Field guide illustrations won't come alive any
    more. Someone perfectly credible tells us
    something totally impossible – making us feel
    more alone. Our holy book is the migration atlas
    which charts individuals: it's possible, just.
    Ignore the runes. Find the rupture in the seal and
    make it whistle.

Exhausted street jewellers, when we doze we spill
from our trays all the rolling beads of our days.

One after another, probably – lightyears travelled on
the lightest meal. Our ending, transpiring
after all, is a headline-grabbing robbery, a night
of splintered crystal. The inveterate slowcoach
tracks the mollusc in its mile, yet suddenly there
it is, the melodrama, the minute broken out of
its gold cage, bars cut and splayed, leaving an
empty page.

Mind isn't owned, it's rented,
    on a ninety-nine-year lease.
Yet not one single bill's resented.
Call off the thought police,
    we'll all undress in public in the end.
Go lightly among the demented.
    Be their echo and their friend.

Love isn't saved, it's squandered,
    and that's how it ought to be.
Down all those coastal lanes we wandered
yet we never glimpsed the sea,
    though almost everyone we met
was carrying swimming things. We wondered,
    can it be far if their hair's still dripping wet?

Past isn't boxed, it's vented,
    and the vapours shuffled round.
It's a rocket-ship they've entered
that they're flying from the ground.
    The carers bring you tea – your favourite blend.
Go lightly among the demented.
    Be their echo and their friend.

Moon Harvest

Earth Life

Two pages from an atlas of sorrow

Vesuvius

'Seraphim flutter around a volcano like moths around a lantern,
and no less precariously.'

*Gazing with terror upon the huge black cloud shaped like
an umbrella pine, the canopy in one fluid motion billowing
outwards, slipping around its trunk and tumbling towards
us down the flanks of the mountain, even so we could
never think of our own safety while we were uncertain of
yours.*

*You, meanwhile, were ready to meet your death in
the satisfaction of knowing that you had not brought our death
any nearer.*

Many centuries later archaeologists took inspiration from
the industrial arts of pottery after discovering in
hardened ash the cavities left by dozens of decomposed
bodies, which they now filled with plaster to recreate
the victims as they had been frozen at the time of
their immolation, like golems awoken to their
inescapable dumb service of espionage and
housework in the ghetto of Prague.

Such grotesquely impertinent pastiches of resurrection
send shockwaves through the afterlife.

Prague

'Good people in exile, never despair. When the greatest day comes,
the Holy One will excavate the land in front of you and your bodies will roll
like bottles into Israel.'

In one of the shacks of the garrison a light was on,
*   and I could hear someone weeping inside.*
Quietly I knocked on the door, and was let in by a rabbi who
*   told me that he had been conscripted to*
*   this establishment as a prison-guard. The springs of*
*   his misery were easily imagined. But in fact*
*   his superior officers had shown him nothing but kindness,*
*   and had reserved this room for him as a secluded study.*
*   Why, then, was he crying?*

'I have been moved to tears while reading the Psalms,
    and thinking of the destruction of the Temple.'

On the golem's forehead was daubed 'Aemaeth',
    meaning Truth, or God, which made him animate.
To put an end to his life of service it was necessary
    to erase the first two letters, leaving 'Maeth',
    meaning Death.
What was *his service?*
To relieve the labours of the poor and defend townspeople
    from the charge of having murdered Christian children
    to furnish with their blood our Passover rituals.

The outside wall of our destiny is blank and white,
    in a rough neighbourhood.
Inside, we decipher the meticulous graffiti of our allegiance.

Lovers of Lanes

That shepherd, sitting cross-legged on La Rocca degli Angeli,
    is a gap-year student whose parents are filthy rich.
His sheep are far below, safe on their aprons of hillside pasture,
    nibbling.
He is at ease in the smock and sandals of a peasant.
He is deep in a book, *The Permanent Instruction of the Alta Vendita:*
    A Masonic Blueprint for the Subversion of the Catholic Church.
From time to time he leans into a thought, lifting his eyes
    towards the seven city hills, folded by lovers of lanes –
    relief from the page this moonlight makes so difficult.

But who are these lovers of lanes, you might be wondering,
    and what have they to do with students, sheep and
    the coiled serpent of enlightenment at the heart of the
    Vatican?
They are the secret custodians of beauty,
    camping among fireflies, brewing up at sundown,
    sleeping in a torrent of dew.
They raise one eyebrow at a stranger's smile.
Their farms have marble inlays and their crumbling villas pigsties.
They are soulful, sensible, without envy and mostly without guile.

Camping on the Moon

It's bedtime, and I'm in disgrace
    with Micro Man and Pudding Face.
I've no Mohicans in my sights –
    I've forfeited my story rights.
No jellyfish kiss has plopped my cheek,
    making the friendly floorboard creak.
The nightlight's off, the landing's dark.
    Outside I hear the werewolves bark.
I'm a castaway in a fool's lagoon.
        I'm camping on the moon.

A rain-soaked pillow slaps my face –
    piss-awful weather, even for space.
Disaster and Bollocks – Gemini –
    swing in their orbit, safe and dry.
The stars are needles, fierce and cold.
    I'm a slave at market, soiled, unsold.
Next door the Joneses rattle their bed,
    moaning and swearing like the living dead.
I'm wide awake in a cruel cartoon.
        I'm camping on the moon.

Downstairs I hear the Bitchlings start,
    the clan the alien tore apart.
I'm a scar, an itch, a boil, a leak.
    I cost a hundred pounds a week.
A mastodon of giant girth,
    I've waddled here to threaten Earth.
I'm swimming in the bed I've wet.
    I'm an animal – so call the vet,
I'm choking to death on a giant spoon.
        I'm camping on the moon.

Iceland

for Peggy – in memory of Eric Ravilious (1903–1942)

Iceland catnaps in levels of milky light,
dramatising your twin pilots of our planet.
Their thoughtfulness makes a feather of a ton
of rock, molten and young, and another
feather of a minke whale to starboard.
A whale's play with an aeroplane can be rough,

as a growing landscape's dreams are rough.
Bear cubs low down are bruisers, bantam-light,
and one stray paw can bat life overboard,
dangle into battle our only planet.
The moon, high-stepping foal, leases from another,
vaster harbour of loneliness. Only a ton

or so, this moon snorts light with wanton
mischief, floating like a smell, lowering rough
cheeks to passion while mourning another –
an artist drowned in a silver web of light.
It's a road without Samaritans, a wild planet –
though in your heart a star of bed and board

ignites eiderdown torches brought to the board
whose sky's a corrugated roof a ton
of meteorites weighs down, held by a fishing net.
Planets go astray like golfballs in the rough
no skill can coax back home in merciless light,
a furnace melting one metal to another.

Yet this, for now, is heath to you, another
warped land of giants all too often bored.
A traveller with a bundle, starved of starlight,
looms from some cosmic myth, like Whittington.
Icelandic kids – shamanic and cool – rough
out raw wisdom just in time to steady the planet

for your passage, heartening as a new planet,
through a wreckage of abolished midnight, another
Babel towering, then tumbling into the rough
flotilla of alpines piping the moon on board,
and two angels, and behind them a singleton,
pied mayor-to-be, fading into councils of light –

rough compensations. One family's bare cupboard
is another family's invisible skeleton.
Turn again. Every planet has its own daylight.

Liberty Hall

A subsided landscape –
             miners break its tombs.
Eve has an infinite
             choice of rhymes,
Adam an infinite
             choice of bedtimes.
Alone in their house,
             I have a choice of rooms.

Warren Lodges

Theberton, Suffolk, May 2005

We wake inside a carapace of pine,
the brain-room cladding nailed up by the dawn,
a backwoods dream distilled, inverted – porn.

Too plausible to prompt a shriek or groan,
the poisoned puddle in an English lane
re-maps the seas and craters of the grain.

Lost in these swirls we feel somewhat unwell,
the bathroom no more soothing than the hall.
A perspex shield sees through you on the wall.

Such wards of wood unbutton to the nurse
whose strip has long since tossed aside its tease.
Longevity, pokerworked in Japanese,

I've wished for you, wrinkled samurai,
who needs a prayer for every doubtful door,
the pine so seasoned and the wind so raw.

Double Trouble

Trouble's got its teeth right into your mind,
    it's a classic consternation blues.
Your momma's dead, and your papa's dying,
        and they're blaring out your secrets on the six o'clock news.
           Folk are hollering like gibbons.
           Slash your troubles into ribbons
    and hang them on the weeping willow trees.
           Don't wipe your eye,
           it's your turn to cry.
I always meant to tell you there'd be days like these.

Trouble's your boss and worry's your wife,
    and they beat you down to moondust like a slave.
They're chewing up your fingers and they're biting off your toes.
        There's a grim and grizzly welcome in the grave.
           Devils hassle you like ghouls,
           and they've ripped up all the rules,
    and you're locked out of your mind without your keys.
           Momma's just a dream,
           Papa's weak as steam.
I always meant to tell you there'd be days like these.

Your camellia's in flower, you got bluetits on your feeder,
    and there ain't no more mosses in your lawn.
But your momma's dead, and your papa's dying,
        and your life would be sweeter if you'd never been born.
           For as long as you're still crying,
           your friends are all still trying,
    whispering good advice in Japanese.
           Down comes the rain,
           crashing through your windowpane.
I always meant to tell you there'd be days like these.

The Firebird

With shimmer of golden wings
    and shudder of crimson tail
she rushes the folded night
    and drapes the trees with smiles,
the many-candled chandelier.
And what she doesn't want she flings
    in the world's face, like hail,
revenge of thwarted appetite,
    dangerous moult of tiles,
the lady bountiful mutineer.

She keeps a leopard as her friend,
    a monkey and two Russian bears,
sedated by a wild Mongolian lay.
    The leopard has a crooked nose,
glamour of damaged goods.
And what she breaks no one can mend.
    It isn't broken then, she swears.
Her day is night, her night is day.
    Her feathers shiver to repose,
on the exact branch in the woods.

Pirate of golden apples patrolled
    by the grey wolf, silently she slides
into the shadows where she herself
    's an apple to the ravenous snake.
Licensed by Eve to roam,
she lives on bugs in leaf-mould,
    purses dropped by brides
in flight from the uninvited wolf,
    and all those crumbs of cake
two children trailed far from home.

A cold moon rinses its light
      in the orchard's dewy bowl,
and somewhere there, aloft,
      ruminating contentedly
in paradise, she consorts
with leaves that quietly recite
      their rubaiyat from the scroll
of themselves, fluttering soft
      in the wind. She watches over me,
and dives into my thoughts.

Selected titles from the Oxford*Poets* list

Oxford*Poets*, an imprint of Carcanet Press, celebrates the vitality and diversity of contemporary poetry in English.

Joseph Brodsky *Collected Poems in English*
For Brodsky, to be a poet was an absolute, a total necessity...scintillating deployment of language, and always tangential or odd ways of interpreting ideas, events or other literature. John Kinsella, OBSERVER

Greg Delanty *Collected Poems 1986–2006*
A body of work that has grown steadily from book to book in depth, invention, and ambition. AGENDA

Jane Draycott *The Night Tree*
Hers is a scrupulous intelligence...Her searching curiosity and wonderful assurance make her an impeccable and central poetic intelligence. Penelope Shuttle, MANHATTAN REVIEW

Sasha Dugdale *The Estate*
Dugdale creates a spare, mythical tone that fits itself perfectly to the elemental Russian landscape in which much of her collection is set. GUARDIAN

Rebecca Elson *A Responsibility to Awe*
This is a wise and haunting volume, which I can't recommend too warmly. Boyd Tonkin, INDEPENDENT

Marilyn Hacker *Essays on Departure*
Everything is thrilling and true, fast and witty, deep and wise; her vitality is the pulse of life itself. Derek Mahon

Peter Scupham *Collected Poems*
The sophistication of the technique which underpins every poem becomes clearer and clearer as you read further in this substantial, generous, distinguished volume. Peter Davidson, Books of the Year 2005, READYSTEADYBOOK.COM

Charles Tomlinson *Cracks in the Universe*
Tomlinson is a unique voice in contemporary English poetry, and has been a satellite of excellence for the past 50 years. David Morley, GUARDIAN

Marina Tsvetaeva *Selected Poems*, trans. **Elaine Feinstein**
Feinstein has performed the first, indispensable task of a great translator: she has captured a voice. THREEPENNY REVIEW

Chris Wallace-Crabbe *By and Large*
His allies are words, and he sues them with the care of a surgeon and the flair of a conjuror. Peter Porter

---